THE MANUAL

THE
MANUAL
EPICTETUS' GUIDE
to STOIC PHILOSOPHY

IF IT'S BEYOND YOUR POWER, LET IT GO.

ADAPTED BY
Sam Torode

ILLUSTRATED BY
Alexander Marchand

THERE ARE THINGS THAT ARE WITHIN YOUR POWER, AND THINGS THAT ARE BEYOND YOUR POWER. THE KEY IS LEARNING TO DISTINGUISH BETWEEN THE TWO.

WITHIN YOUR POWER ARE YOUR OPINIONS, DESIRES—THE THINGS YOU PURSUE—AVERSIONS—THE THINGS YOU AVOID—AND HOW YOU TREAT OTHER PEOPLE. IN SUM, **YOUR OWN THOUGHTS AND ACTIONS.**

BEYOND YOUR POWER ARE YOUR FAMILY AND NATIONALITY, THE PHYSICAL CHARACTERISTICS YOU WERE BORN WITH, THE THOUGHTS AND ACTIONS OF **OTHERS**, AND ALL THAT **FATE** MAY GIVE OR TAKE FROM YOU.

WITHIN YOUR **SPHERE OF POWER,** YOU'RE FREE, INDEPENDENT, AND STRONG. **OUTSIDE** THAT SPHERE, YOU'RE CONSTRAINED, DEPENDENT, AND WEAK.

1

IF YOU PIN YOUR HOPES ON THINGS **OUTSIDE YOUR CONTROL**, YOU'RE LIKELY TO END UP **MISERABLE**, BLAMING OTHERS AND CURSING THE GODS.

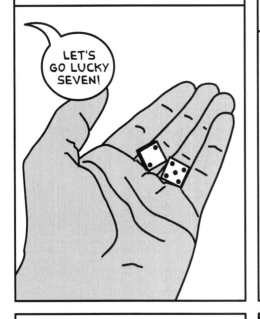

LET'S GO LUCKY SEVEN!

BUT IF YOU FOCUS ONLY ON WHAT'S WITHIN YOUR POWER, THEN **YOU'RE IN CHARGE**. WHEN YOU TAKE RESPONSIBILITY FOR YOUR OWN THOUGHTS AND ACTIONS, THERE'S NO ONE TO BLAME OR FIGHT.

WITHIN YOUR POWER

REMEMBER THAT YOUR **THOUGHTS** ARE **NOT FACTS**; THEY'RE **INTERPRETATIONS**. WHENEVER SOMETHING UPSETS YOU, ASK: "IS THIS INSIDE OR OUTSIDE MY SPHERE OF POWER?" AND IF IT'S BEYOND YOUR POWER, **LET IT GO**.

IS THIS INSIDE OR OUTSIDE MY SPHERE OF POWER?

* SYMBOL FOR **SPHERE OF POWER**

II

DESIRE DRIVES YOU TO **ACQUIRE** THINGS. **AVERSION** DRIVES YOU TO **AVOID** THINGS. WHEN YOU DON'T GET WHAT YOU WANT, YOU'RE **DISAPPOINTED**. WHEN YOU GET WHAT YOU DON'T WANT, YOU'RE **DISTRESSED**.

BY STRIVING TO ATTAIN OR AVOID THINGS THAT ARE BEYOND YOUR CONTROL, YOU INFLICT **MENTAL ANGUISH** UPON YOURSELF.

IF IT DOESN'T RAIN SOON, I'M GOING TO LOSE THE CROP.

LEARN TO **DIRECT** YOUR DESIRE AND AVERSION TO THINGS THAT ARE **WITHIN YOUR POWER**, AND TAKE A **NEUTRAL ATTITUDE** TO EVERYTHING ELSE. THEN YOU'LL BE CONTENT.

GIVEN THE DRY WEATHER, IT'S A GOOD THING THE FARM HAS AN IRRIGATION SYSTEM.

FOR INSTANCE, INSTEAD OF DESIRING **FAME** AND **WEALTH**, DESIRE TO IMPROVE YOUR **CHARACTER** AND **WORK ETHIC**. AND INSTEAD OF **WORRYING** ABOUT SICKNESS OR DEATH, TAKE UP HEALTHY HABITS AND **LET GO OF FEAR**.

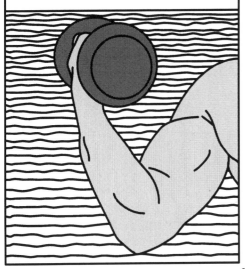

FIRST, SECURE YOUR SPHERE OF POWER. **THEN** YOU MAY CHOOSE TO PURSUE SOMETHING OUTSIDE YOUR CONTROL—SUCH AS STRIVING TO WIN A COMPETITION—WITH **CALM DETERMINATION**. WIN OR LOSE, YOU WON'T BE INFLATED OR CRUSHED BY THE OUTCOME.

III

WHAT ABOUT **POSSESSIONS** YOU ENJOY, OR **PEOPLE** THAT YOU LOVE? SINCE THEY'RE OUTSIDE YOUR CONTROL, SHOULD YOU **DETACH** FROM THEM?

NO, IT'S GOOD TO **LOVE** AND **APPRECIATE** THE BLESSINGS IN YOUR LIFE. JUST **REMIND YOURSELF** OF THEIR NATURE.

WHEN YOU DRINK FROM YOUR FAVORITE CUP, **REMEMBER** THAT IT'S MADE OF CLAY. IF IT WERE TO BREAK, YOU COULD BEAR IT.

WHEN YOU HUG YOUR LOVED ONES, **REMEMBER** THAT THEY'RE MORTAL. ACCEPT THEIR NATURE RATHER THAN DENYING IT. THEN, IF THEY DIE, YOU'LL FIND THE STRENGTH TO BEAR IT.

IV

LIKEWISE, WHEN YOU PREPARE FOR ANY **ACTION** OR **EVENT**, REMIND YOURSELF OF ITS **NATURE**.

FOR INSTANCE, BEFORE GOING TO THE PUBLIC POOL, **THINK** OF WHAT USUALLY HAPPENS: PEOPLE ARE NOISY, KIDS ARE SPLASHING, AND UNATTENDED ITEMS ARE LIABLE TO BE STOLEN. SET YOUR **EXPECTATIONS** ACCORDINGLY, AND YOU WON'T BE DISAPPOINTED.

IF SOMETHING UNDESIRABLE HAPPENS—SUCH AS YOU GET SPLASHED IN THE FACE—REMIND YOURSELF,

MY DESIRE IS TO STAY IN **HARMONY** WITH THE NATURE OF THINGS. AND THAT PERSON'S NATURE IS TO SPLASH.

V

PEOPLE AREN'T UPSET BY **THINGS THEMSELVES**, BUT BY THE **OPINIONS** THEY HAVE OF THOSE THINGS.

EVEN DEATH, IN ITSELF, IS NOTHING TO FEAR. THE **FEAR** OF DEATH COMES FROM THE **OPINION** THAT DEATH IS HORRIFIC.

NOTHING TO FEAR

SOCRATES HAD A DIFFERENT OPINION. HE VIEWED DEATH AS A **RETURN TO THE SOURCE**. HE CHOSE TO DIE RATHER THAN BETRAY HIS PRINCIPLES, WHICH—TO HIM—WOULD HAVE BEEN THE **REAL** TRAGEDY.

WHEN YOU'RE UPSET, ANGRY, OR SAD, DON'T BLAME ANYONE ELSE. YOUR **STATE OF MIND** COMES FROM YOUR OWN **OPINIONS** AND **INTERPRETATIONS**.

THOSE WHO ARE **IGNORANT** OF PHILOSOPHY BLAME FATE OR OTHER PEOPLE FOR THEIR OWN CONDITION. THOSE WHO ARE **BEGINNING TO LEARN** PHILOSOPHY BLAME THEMSELVES. THOSE WHO HAVE **MASTERED** PHILOSOPHY BLAME NO ONE.

DON'T TAKE PRIDE IN POSSESSIONS—THEY'RE NOT REALLY YOURS.

IF A HORSE WERE TO SAY, "LOOK AT ME—I'M SO HANDSOME!" HIS VANITY MAY BE EXCUSABLE.

BUT IF **YOU** BRAG, "I HAVE THE HANDSOMEST HORSE IN THE LAND," YOU'RE CLAIMING MERIT THAT DOESN'T BELONG TO YOU.

WHAT IS **TRULY YOURS**? YOUR OWN **THOUGHTS**, **WORDS**, AND **ACTIONS**. WHEN THESE ARE **IN HARMONY**, YOU CAN TAKE JUST SATISFACTION.

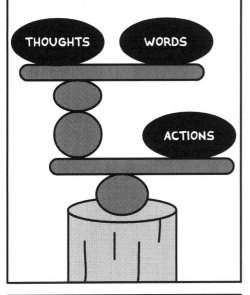

VII

IMAGINE YOU'RE TAKING A **SEA VOYAGE**. WHILE THE SHIP IS ANCHORED AND YOU GO ASHORE FOR SUPPLIES, YOU MAY AMUSE YOURSELF BY LOOKING FOR BEAUTIFUL SHELLS AND STONES ON THE BEACH.

BUT ALWAYS KEEP PART OF YOUR MIND **FOCUSED** ON THE SHIP AND **STAY ALERT** FOR THE CAPTAIN'S CALL. BE PREPARED TO DROP YOUR "TREASURES," OR YOU MAY MISS THE BOAT!

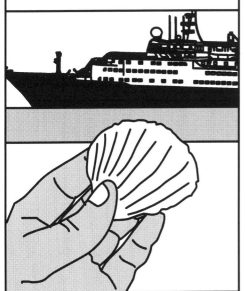

SO IN LIFE, REMAIN **STEADFAST** IN **PURSUIT OF YOUR MISSION**, ALWAYS WILLING TO SHED DISTRACTIONS.

7

VIII

DON'T WISH THAT ALL THINGS WILL GO WELL WITH YOU, BUT THAT **YOU** WILL GO WELL WITH ALL THINGS.

EACH TIME AN OBSTACLE ARISES, REMIND YOURSELF OF THIS TRUTH: WHILE IT MAY HURT SOME PART OF YOU, IT CAN'T TOUCH YOUR **DEEPEST SELF**.

IX

LAMENESS MAY STRIKE YOUR LEG, BUT NOT YOUR **DETERMINATION**. SICKNESS MAY WEAKEN YOUR BODY, BUT NOT YOUR **CHARACTER**. MISFORTUNE MAY DRAIN YOUR BANK ACCOUNT, BUT NOT YOUR **GENEROSITY**— UNLESS YOU LET IT.

THE **ONLY PERSON** WHO CAN TRULY HARM YOU—THAT IS, MAKE YOU A WORSE PERSON—IS **YOU**.

X

WHENEVER YOU FACE A CHALLENGE, TURN INWARD AND ASK...

WHAT **POWER** CAN I EXERCISE IN THIS SITUATION?

IF YOU MEET TEMPTATION, EXERCISE **SELF CONTROL**. IF YOU MEET PAIN, EXERCISE **PERSEVERANCE**. IF YOU MEET FRUSTRATION, EXERCISE **PATIENCE**.

SELF CONTROL

OUCH! PAPER CUT!

PERSEVERANCE

WILL THIS LIGHT EVER CHANGE?

PATIENCE

BY DOING THIS REPEATEDLY, YOU'LL GAIN STRENGTH TO **OVERCOME** LIFE'S CHALLENGES RATHER THAN BE OVERCOME **BY THEM**.

XI

DON'T SAY OF ANYTHING, "I'VE LOST IT," BUT RATHER, **"I'VE GIVEN IT BACK."**

DID YOUR CUP FALL AND SHATTER? YOU'VE GIVEN IT BACK. DID SOMEONE STEAL YOUR JEWELRY? YOU'VE GIVEN IT BACK. DID YOUR GRANDMOTHER PASS AWAY? YOU'VE GIVEN HER BACK.

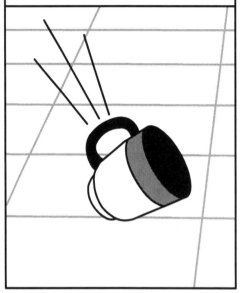

TREAT EVERYTHING AS THOUGH IT WERE **ON LOAN**, BECAUSE IT IS. EVENTUALLY, ALL THINGS MUST RETURN TO THEIR **DIVINE SOURCE**. THE METHOD AND TIMING OF THEIR RETURN IS NOT UP TO YOU.

XII

EXCUSES

IF YOU WANT TO MOVE FORWARD, **PUT ASIDE YOUR EXCUSES**.

BUT IF I DON'T CLING TO MY POSSESSIONS, SOMEONE WILL STEAL THEM!

AND IF I DON'T WORRY ABOUT MONEY, I'LL END UP ON THE STREET!

ENOUGH WITH THE CATASTROPHIZING. WHAT'S BETTER: TO DIE POOR YET **FREE FROM FEAR**, OR TO LIVE SURROUNDED BY RICHES YET **FILLED WITH ANXIETY?**

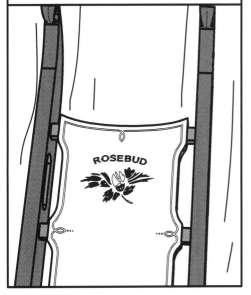

START WITH **SMALL THINGS**. IF A BOTTLE OF WINE IS BROKEN OR GOES MISSING, REMIND YOURSELF, "ACCEPTING SUCH ANNOYANCES IS THE **PRICE** OF MY **PEACE OF MIND.**"

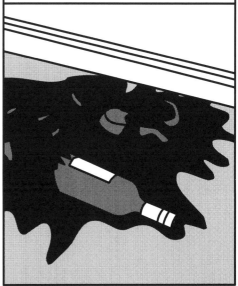

OR IF YOU ASK A FRIEND TO DO SOMETHING AND THEY DON'T, REMEMBER THAT **THEY'RE RESPONSIBLE** FOR THEIR OWN ACTIONS. WHY GIVE THEM THE POWER TO UPSET YOU?

DID YOU BRING BACK MY BOOK?

SLIPPED MY MIND.

XIII

AS YOU EMBARK ON THE **PATH OF PHILOSOPHY**, DON'T MIND WHAT OTHERS MAY THINK ABOUT YOU— EVEN IF THEY CALL YOU FOOLISH. DON'T EXPECT TO BE PRAISED FOR PURSUING PEACE.

AND IF YOU ARE PRAISED BY OTHERS, BE **SKEPTICAL** OF YOURSELF. IT'S NO EASY FEAT TO HOLD ONTO YOUR INNER HARMONY WHILE COLLECTING ACCOLADES! WHEN GRASPING FOR ONE, YOU'RE LIKELY TO DROP THE OTHER.

XIV

IT WOULD BE FOOLISH TO EXPECT YOUR FAMILY AND FRIENDS TO LIVE FOREVER. THEIR LIVES ARE NOT IN YOUR POWER.

IT'S ALSO FOOLISH TO EXPECT THEM TO BE PERFECT AND TO ALWAYS PLEASE YOU. DON'T WISH SOMEONE TO BE SOMETHING THEY'RE NOT.

WHENEVER YOU STRONGLY DESIRE SOMETHING THAT'S BEYOND YOUR CONTROL, YOU SET YOURSELF UP FOR **DISAPPOINTMENT**. TO AVOID DISAPPOINTMENT, DIRECT YOUR DESIRES TO THINGS THAT ARE WITHIN YOUR **SPHERE OF POWER**.

IF YOU WISH TO BE **FREE**, DON'T PIN YOUR HAPPINESS ON ANYONE ELSE, OR YOU'LL MAKE THEM YOUR MASTER.

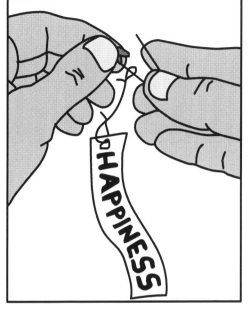

APPROACH LIFE AS A BANQUET. AS EACH PLATTER IS PASSED TO YOU, SAMPLE IT WITH **GRATITUDE**. IF YOU'RE WAITING FOR YOUR FAVORITE DISH TO COME AROUND, DON'T LUNGE ACROSS THE TABLE FOR IT—**BE PATIENT**.

AND IF THE PLATE IS EMPTY WHEN IT REACHES YOU, DON'T GRUMBLE. INSTEAD, BE GLAD THAT OTHERS WERE ABLE TO ENJOY IT.

IF YOU TREAT EVERYTHING IN LIFE THIS WAY, YOU'LL BE WORTHY TO **FEAST WITH THE GODS!**

XVI

LEARN TO DISTINGUISH BETWEEN **EVENTS** AND **INTERPRETATIONS**. EVENTS THEMSELVES DO NOT UPSET US. RATHER, IT'S THE **STORIES WE TELL OURSELVES** ABOUT THOSE EVENTS.

ONE ATHLETE MAY BE DISTRAUGHT OVER A SETBACK AND GIVE UP; WHILE ANOTHER MAY BE SPURRED ON, EAGER TO OVERCOME THE CHALLENGE.

WHEN YOU SEE SOMEONE GRIEVING, ASK YOURSELF WHAT STORY IS BEHIND THEIR TEARS. IF THEY LOOKED AT THINGS FROM A **DIFFERENT PERSPECTIVE**, WOULD IT CHANGE THEIR FEELINGS?

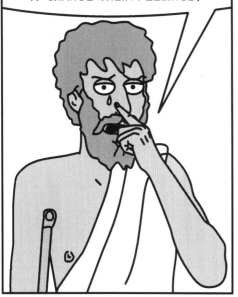

DON'T SHARE YOUR THOUGHTS WITH THE GRIEVING PERSON, UNLESS ASKED. ONLY **SYMPATHIZE** WITH THEM, AND EVEN CRY WITH THEM. YOUR TEARS WILL BE OUTWARD, WHILE INWARDLY YOU REMAIN AT PEACE.

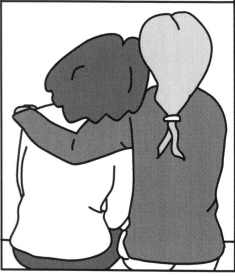

XVII

YOUR
LIFE

THINK OF LIFE AS A **PLAY**, AND YOURSELF AS AN ACTOR. THE ROLE YOU PLAY, AND THE AMOUNT OF TIME YOU HAVE ON THE STAGE, IS NOT UP TO YOU—IT'S UP TO THE **AUTHOR**.

YOU MAY BE CAST AS A PAUPER, A CRIPPLE, OR A KING. YOU DIDN'T CHOOSE THE ERA, NATIONALITY, CLASS, FAMILY, OR BODY INTO WHICH YOU WERE BORN.

BUT YOU ALONE HAVE THE POWER TO ACT WELL IN YOUR ROLE. **PLAY YOUR PART** TO THE BEST OF YOUR ABILITY!

XVIII

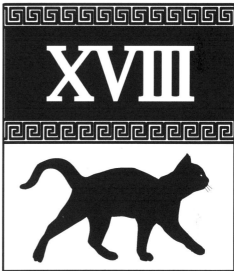

IF YOU BREAK A MIRROR OR A BLACK CAT CROSSES YOUR PATH, DON'T LET **FEAR OF BAD LUCK** CREATE A SELF-FULFILLING PROPHECY. "BAD OMENS" HAVE **NO POWER** UNLESS WE GIVE IT TO THEM.

REMIND YOURSELF, "ALL SIGNS POINT TO **GOOD LUCK** IF I INTERPRET THEM THAT WAY. I'LL **FIND THE ADVANTAGE** IN EVERYTHING THAT COMES MY WAY."

XIX

IF YOU LEARN TO **ACCEPT** ALL THINGS THAT ARE OUTSIDE YOUR CONTROL, INSTEAD OF **RESISTING** THEM, YOU'LL BE UNSHAKABLE.

WHEN YOU SEE A PERSON WHO'S RICH, FAMOUS, OR POWERFUL, DON'T BE TAKEN IN BY APPEARANCES AND ASSUME THAT THEY'RE HAPPY.

WHEN YOU FOCUS ON **CULTIVATING YOUR OWN VIRTUE**, THERE'S NO ROOM FOR ENVYING OR IMITATING OTHERS. INSTEAD OF DESIRING TO BE A BILLIONAIRE, A CELEBRITY, OR A PRESIDENT, DESIRE TO BE **FREE**.

AND THE WAY TO BE FREE IS TO WORK WITHIN YOUR SPHERE OF POWER, AND LET GO OF EVERYTHING OUTSIDE YOUR CONTROL.

XX

WHEN SOMEONE UPSETS YOU, REMEMBER THAT IT'S ACTUALLY **YOUR OWN OPINION** THAT UPSETS YOU.

IT'S NOT THE PERSON WHO CRITICIZES OR ATTACKS YOU WHO TORMENTS YOUR MIND, BUT THE **STORY** YOU TELL YOURSELF ABOUT WHAT HAS HAPPENED.

DON'T BE FOOLED BY THE FIRST STORY THAT ENTERS YOUR MIND. GIVE IT **TIME** AND SEEK A **WIDER PERSPECTIVE**. THEN YOU'LL REGAIN INNER PEACE.

XXI

EVERY DAY, REMIND YOURSELF THAT YOU'RE A **MORTAL BEING** AND YOUR TIME ON EARTH IS LIMITED.

INSTEAD OF DEPRESSING YOU, THIS IS MEANT TO **INSPIRE YOU** TO USE YOUR **PRECIOUS TIME** WISELY, AND NOT WASTE IT IN CHASING AFTER THINGS OR STEWING OVER GRIEVANCES.

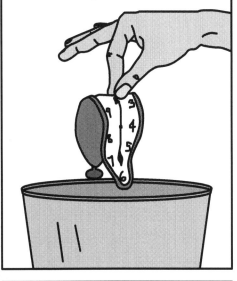

XXII

IF YOU INTEND TO FOLLOW THE PATH OF PHILOSOPHY, EXPECT YOUR FAMILY AND FRIENDS TO **MISUNDERSTAND** OR **MOCK** YOU.

WELL, WELL, LOOK WHO'S A PHILOSOPHER NOW!

SO, YOU THINK YOU'RE BETTER THAN US?

DON'T ARGUE WITH THEM OR TAKE ON AN AIR OF SUPERIORITY. SIMPLY **STAY FOCUSED** ON YOUR INNER WORK, WHILE PERFORMING YOUR OUTER WORK—AT SCHOOL, IN YOUR JOB, WHEREVER YOU ARE—TO THE BEST OF YOUR ABILITY.

IF YOU ABANDON THE PATH TO PLEASE OTHERS, YOU MIGHT **AVOID CRITICISM** BUT **BETRAY YOURSELF.**

XXIII

DETOUR →

WHENEVER YOU FIND YOURSELF ACTING TO IMPRESS OTHERS, OR STOPPING OUT OF FEAR OF WHAT OTHERS MIGHT THINK, YOU'VE **LEFT THE PATH.**

FIND SATISFACTION IN **SEEKING WISDOM** AND **CULTIVATING VIRTUE**—NOT IN PRAISE AND HONORS.

IF YOU WANT TO BE RESPECTED, START BY RESPECTING **YOURSELF!**

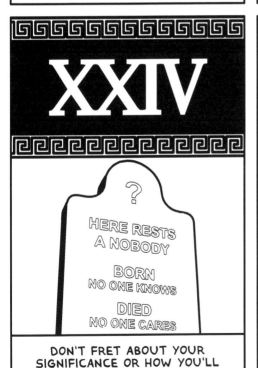

XXIV

HERE RESTS A NOBODY

BORN NO ONE KNOWS

DIED NO ONE CARES

DON'T FRET ABOUT YOUR SIGNIFICANCE OR HOW YOU'LL BE REMEMBERED.

I'LL NEVER BE ANYBODY. I'M JUST A NOBODY FROM NOWHERE.

INSTEAD OF STRIVING FOR FAME AND RENOWN, FIND YOUR SIGNIFICANCE WITHIN **YOURSELF.**

BUT I WANT FAME SO THAT I CAN REACH A LARGE AUDIENCE AND HELP OTHERS.

WHAT DO YOU MEAN BY "HELP"? CAN YOU REALLY GIVE THEM HAPPINESS AND PEACE OF MIND? THAT'S WITHIN **THEIR** SPHERE OF POWER, NOT YOURS. AND EVEN IF IT WERE POSSIBLE—HOW CAN YOU GIVE SOMEONE A GIFT THAT YOU, YOURSELF, DON'T HAVE?

IF YOU CAN ACCUMULATE RICHES WITHOUT SACRIFICING YOUR HONOR AND SELF-RESPECT, THEN DO IT. BUT IF YOU **COMPROMISE YOUR PRINCIPLES** IN THE PROCESS, NO AMOUNT OF MONEY CAN MAKE UP FOR LOST VIRTUE.

WHICH WOULD YOU RATHER HAVE— MONEY TO GIVE AWAY, OR LOYAL AND TRUSTWORTHY FRIENDS? THE TWO DON'T OFTEN GO TOGETHER.

TO BECOME THE KIND OF PERSON WHO **ATTRACTS** GOOD FRIENDS, BUILD YOUR **CHARACTER**—NOT YOUR BANK ACCOUNT.

THEN WHAT'S MY ROLE IN THE WORLD?

THE ONE IN WHICH YOU CAN BEST EXPRESS YOUR **TALENTS AND SKILLS**, WHICH ARE WITHIN YOUR SPHERE OF POWER. EVERYONE HAS A **VITAL ROLE** TO PLAY—YOU'RE ALREADY IMPORTANT, RIGHT WHERE YOU ARE.

XXV

DO YOU ENVY SOMEONE WHO'S POPULAR AND GETS INVITED TO ALL THE BEST PARTIES? IF THEY'RE ADMIRED BECAUSE OF THEIR **VIRTUE**, BE GLAD FOR THEM. BUT IF THEY'RE CELEBRATED FOR THEIR **VICES**, BE GLAD YOU'RE NOT LIKE THEM.

WHEN YOU SEE SOMEONE WHO'S BELOVED BY MANY, NOTICE THE EFFORT THEY PUT INTO **BUILDING RELATIONSHIPS**. IF YOU WANT TO **HAVE** GOOD FRIENDS, YOU MUST **BE** A GOOD FRIEND.

EVERYTHING HAS ITS **PRICE**. WHEN YOU AREN'T INVITED TO A PARTY, IT'S PROBABLY BECAUSE YOU HAVEN'T SPENT TIME TALKING WITH, ENCOURAGING, AND PRAISING THE HOSTS. IS THAT A PRICE YOU'RE WILLING TO PAY?

NO INVITATION IS WORTH FLATTERING PEOPLE YOU DON'T REALLY ADMIRE AND MAKING SMALL TALK WITH PEOPLE YOU DON'T REALLY LIKE.

XXVI

IF YOUR NEIGHBOR'S CHILD BROKE THEIR PRECIOUS VASE, YOU'D LIKELY SAY—

OH WELL, ACCIDENTS HAPPEN.

BUT HOW WOULD YOU REACT IF A CHILD SHATTERED **YOUR** VASE?

THAT'S BEEN IN THE FAMILY FOR HUNDREDS OF YEARS!

WHY THE DIFFERENCE? YOU OUGHT TO REACT WITH **CALMNESS** AND **UNDERSTANDING** IN BOTH CASES.

WHENEVER MISFORTUNE BEFALLS YOU, ASK YOURSELF—

HOW WOULD I REACT IF **SOMEONE ELSE** WAS IN THIS SITUATION?

XXVII

GOODNESS STANDS BEFORE US LIKE AN ARCHER'S TARGET.

EVIL HAS NO POSITIVE EXISTENCE; IT'S MERELY THE **LACK** OF GOODNESS. SIN IS A **MISSING OF THE MARK**—AN ARROW GONE ASTRAY.

XXVIII

IF SOMEONE TRIED TO CONTROL YOUR **BODY** AND MAKE YOU A SLAVE, YOU'D FIGHT FOR FREEDOM.

BUT HOW EASILY YOU HAND OVER YOUR **MIND** TO THOSE WHO OFFEND OR INSULT YOU! BY CONTINUALLY STEWING OVER THEIR MISDEEDS, YOU MAKE THEM YOUR **MASTER**.

XXIX

WHEN APPROACHING ANY SITUATION, CONSIDER ALL THREE PHASES—BEFORE, DURING, AND AFTER. **THEN TAKE ACTION**. IF YOU ACT WITHOUT CONSIDERING CAUSES AND CONSEQUENCES, YOU'LL FLOUNDER AND FAIL.

LET'S SAY YOU WANT TO ENTER A WRESTLING TOURNAMENT. WHAT COMES **BEFORE**? YOU MUST TRAIN HARD, EAT WELL, AND LISTEN TO YOUR COACH.

WHAT MIGHT HAPPEN **DURING** AND **AFTER** THE TOURNAMENT? DEVISE A GAMEPLAN FOR ALL CONTINGENCIES, INCLUDING POSSIBLE INJURY AND REHABILITATION.

ONCE YOU'VE CONSIDERED ALL THAT MIGHT HAPPEN, IF YOU STILL WANT TO COMPETE, **START TRAINING**. BUT IF YOU HAVEN'T SERIOUSLY THOUGHT THINGS THROUGH, YOU'RE ONLY DAYDREAMING ABOUT BEING A WRESTLER.

BECOMING A PHILOSOPHER, LIKE BECOMING A WRESTLER, TAKES **PRACTICE**. IT ISN'T A HOBBY TO BE DABBLED IN AND ABANDONED WHEN THE GOING GETS TOUGH.

A LOT OF PEOPLE WHO FANCY THEMSELVES PHILOSOPHERS ARE MERE **IMITATORS**. THEY'VE CHANGED THEIR WAY OF DRESSING AND SPEAKING—BUT NOT THEIR **THINKING**. THEY CAN REPEAT WISE WORDS, BUT ON THE INSIDE, THEIR MINDS ARE CAULDRONS OF **FEAR** AND **ENVY**.

IF YOU TRULY WISH TO BE A PHILOSOPHER, YOU MUST GAIN **DISCIPLINE AND SELF-CONTROL**, GIVE UP FRIENDS WHO ARE **BAD INFLUENCES**, STOP STRIVING FOR **POWER, RICHES, AND FAME**, AND WILLINGLY ACCEPT **RIDICULE** AND **SCORN**.

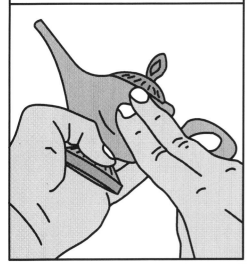

ARE YOU EAGER TO MAKE THESE **SACRIFICES** FOR **PEACE, FREEDOM, AND INNER HARMONY**? IF SO, START TRAINING!

25

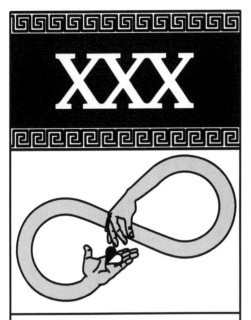

XXX

ALL RELATIONSHIPS COME WITH RECIPROCAL **DUTIES**. PARENTS HAVE THE DUTY TO LOVE, CARE FOR, AND TEACH THEIR CHILDREN.

CHILDREN HAVE THE DUTY OF FOLLOWING THEIR PARENTS' INSTRUCTION, RECEIVING THEIR CORRECTION, AND CARING FOR THEM IN THEIR OLD AGE.

GO PLAY IN THE STREET!

BUT WHAT IF YOUR PARENT GIVES YOU BAD ADVICE, OR TREATS YOU UNFAIRLY—ARE YOUR DUTIES CANCELLED?

BEFORE JUDGING **THEIR** BEHAVIOR—WHICH YOU CAN'T CONTROL—LOOK TO YOUR **OWN**. FULFILL YOUR DUTIES AS BEST YOU CAN WITHOUT COMPROMISING YOUR OWN **DIGNITY** AND **INNER HARMONY**.

IF YOU MUST DISOBEY OR DISAPPOINT A PARENT, DO IT WITH **KIND INTENTIONS** AND A **CLEAR CONSCIENCE**. REMEMBER—NO ONE CAN STEAL YOUR PEACE OF MIND UNLESS YOU LET THEM.

XXXI

TO KNOW THE GODS, STUDY THE **WAYS OF NATURE**. FOLLOW THEM, LET THEM SHAPE YOU, AND BE GUIDED BY THEIR PERFECT WISDOM. STAY CLOSE TO NATURE, AND YOU'LL NEVER FEEL FAR FROM THE GODS.

GO WITH THE FLOW OF NATURE BY LETTING GO OF ALL THINGS BEYOND YOUR CONTROL. DON'T JUDGE THE THINGS THAT COME YOUR WAY AS "GOOD" OR "BAD"—ONLY JUDGE **YOUR OWN** THOUGHTS, DESIRES, AND ACTIONS.

IF YOU **FIGHT THE FLOW**, BY ARGUING WITH EVENTS AND CIRCUMSTANCES OUTSIDE YOUR CONTROL, YOU'LL END UP CURSING THE GODS. FOR IF YOU BELIEVE THE GODS WOULD DELIBERATELY TRY TO HARM YOU, HOW CAN YOU WORSHIP THEM?

FLOW LIKE A FEATHER IN THE WIND.

WHERE YOUR **LOVE** IS, THERE IS YOUR **WORSHIP**. RELIGION ISN'T SOMETHING SET APART FROM THE REST OF LIFE. WORSHIP THE GODS IN **HUMILITY** AND **SIMPLICITY** BY EMBRACING NATURE'S WAYS.

XXXII

IT'S HELPFUL TO ANTICIPATE FUTURE EVENTS AND PLAN FOR THEM; BUT DON'T LET WHAT MIGHT HAPPEN **TOMORROW** MAKE YOU FEARFUL OR ANXIOUS **TODAY**.

THE FUTURE IS BEYOND YOUR CONTROL; BUT IT'S WITHIN YOUR POWER TO APPROACH IT WITH AN **OPEN** AND **PEACEFUL** MIND.

REMEMBER THAT OUTSIDE EVENTS CAN'T TOUCH YOUR DEEPEST SELF—WHAT MATTERS IS HOW YOU **INTERPRET** AND **REACT** TO THEM. WITH THE RIGHT MINDSET, YOU CAN USE **ANY** CIRCUMSTANCE TO YOUR BENEFIT.

TRUST FATE, AND TRUST YOURSELF. **TAKE COUNSEL FROM NATURE**, NOT FROM PROPHETS AND PROGNOSTICATORS.

SUPPOSE YOU VISIT A FORTUNE TELLER, AND SHE PREDICTS THAT ONE OF YOUR FRIENDS WILL BETRAY YOU. WILL YOU LET THIS CHANGE YOUR BEHAVIOR, BY ABANDONING YOUR FRIEND BEFORE THEY CAN ABANDON YOU?

NATURE TEACHES THAT WE'RE ALL **CONNECTED** AND **INTERDEPENDENT**. BEING A **LOYAL FRIEND** IS ITS **OWN REWARD**—IT MAKES YOU A BETTER PERSON—EVEN IF YOUR FRIENDS SOMETIMES LET YOU DOWN. WHAT OTHER ORACLE DO YOU NEED?

BE THE SAME PERSON IN **PUBLIC** AS IN **PRIVATE**.

BE A **GOOD LISTENER**, NOT A LOUDMOUTH OR BORE. SPEAK ONLY WHAT'S **CONSTRUCTIVE** AND **ENRICHING**.

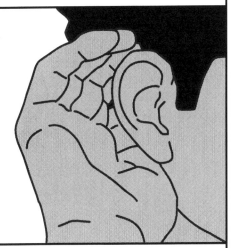

DON'T PARTICIPATE IN **GOSSIP**. WHEN PEOPLE START CRITICIZING AND COMPLAINING, CHANGE THE SUBJECT OR LEAVE THE ROOM.

AVOID DEGRADING ENTERTAINMENT. IF YOUR FRIENDS KEEP INVITING YOU TO WATCH SUCH SHOWS, FIND NEW FRIENDS OR YOU'LL SOON FIND YOURSELF **OFF THE PATH** AND IN A **MUD PIT**.

WHEN YOU ATTEND SPORTING EVENTS, DON'T LET THE OUTCOME DETERMINE YOUR MOOD. APPRECIATE ALL THE ATHLETES' EFFORTS, AND WISH ONLY THAT THE BEST WILL WIN.

WHY WOULD YOU RUN A PASS PLAY ON FOURTH AND INCHES?

AT PARTIES, BE A POLITE GUEST. DON'T DRINK TO THE POINT OF LOSING YOUR DIGNITY.

IF YOU'RE NOT SURE HOW TO ACT, JUST ASK YOURSELF—**WHAT WOULD SOCRATES DO**? MODEL YOURSELF AFTER THE WISEST.

XXXIV

WHEN YOU'RE BURNING WITH **LUST**, YOU'RE LIKE A PERSON UNDER A **SPELL**.

INSTEAD OF ACTING ON IMPULSE, TAKE A STEP BACK. CONSIDER THE **COSTS** OF PURSUING THIS PLEASURE AND WHAT **CONSEQUENCES** MAY FOLLOW. ASK YOURSELF—

HOW WILL I FEEL ABOUT THIS **TOMORROW**?

THEN ASK—"HOW WILL I FEEL ABOUT MYSELF IF I **RESIST** THIS TEMPTATION?"

ASKING THESE QUESTIONS WILL **BREAK THE SPELL**. SOON YOU'LL SEE THINGS AS THEY REALLY ARE.

IF YOU DECIDE THAT A PLEASURE IS WHOLESOME AND HARMLESS, ENJOY IT IN **MODERATION**.

SELF-RESPECT IS MORE SATISFYING THAN ANY BODILY PLEASURE.

XXXV

ONCE YOU'VE THOUGHT THROUGH THE CONSEQUENCES, **ACT DECISIVELY**. DON'T WORRY ABOUT WHAT OTHERS WILL THINK, EVEN IF THE WHOLE WORLD MIGHT MISUNDERSTAND YOU.

IF YOU WIND UP OFF COURSE, **CORRECT YOURSELF**. BUT IF YOU KNOW YOU DID THE RIGHT THING, WHY FEAR THOSE WHO MISJUDGE YOU?

XXXVI

BLACK AND WHITE THINKING MAKES FOR POWERFUL SPEECHES, BUT REAL LIFE IS MOSTLY **SHADES OF GRAY**. IT'S RARELY A QUESTION OF GOOD VERSUS EVIL, BUT OF WEIGHING GREATER AND LESSER GOODS ON A **SCALE OF VALUES**.

AT A BANQUET, TAKING ALL THE CHOICE CUTS MAY BE GOOD FOR YOUR BELLY, BUT SHARING GENEROUSLY IS GOOD FOR THE SPIRIT OF CELEBRATION. WEIGHING THE TWO GOODS, SEEING YOUR FELLOW GUESTS ENJOY THEMSELVES IS **MORE VALUABLE** THAN GRATIFYING YOUR OWN APPETITE.

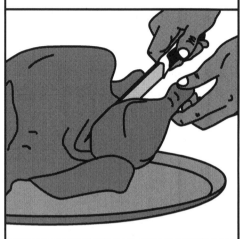

XXXVII

TALENT STACK

| DESIGN |
| ECONOMICS |
| PERSUASION |
| FITNESS |
| WRITING |
| PUBLIC SPEAKING |
| CODING |
| PHILOSOPHY |

MEANINGFUL WORK IS THAT WHICH IS BEST SUITED TO YOUR UNIQUE GIFTS.

IF YOU PRETEND TO BE SOMEONE YOU'RE NOT, YOU MIGHT GAIN FAME, RICHES, OR POLITICAL POWER—BUT YOU'LL MISS OUT ON THE JOYS OF A LIFE SPENT EXPRESSING YOUR **TRUE THOUGHTS**, **TEMPERAMENT**, AND **TALENTS**.

JUST TELL ME WHAT I NEED TO SAY AND DO TO GET ELECTED AND I'LL SAY AND DO THAT.

XXXVIII

WHEN WALKING IN THE WOODS, WATCH FOR SHARP STONES AND FALLEN BRANCHES IN YOUR PATH.

SO, TOO, WHEN THINKING—TAKE CARE NOT TO STUMBLE INTO **ILLOGIC** AND **UNREASON**.

XXXIX

OUR POSSESSIONS SHOULD BE **SUITED TO OUR NEEDS**, JUST AS OUR SHOES ARE SUITED TO OUR FEET.

COULD YOU RUN FASTER IF YOUR SHOES WERE **LARGER** THAN YOUR FEET, OR GOLD-PLATED AND DIAMOND STUDDED? OF COURSE NOT.

ONCE YOU LET YOUR APPETITE EXCEED WHAT IS **NECESSARY** AND **HELPFUL**, DESIRE KNOWS NO BOUNDS.

XL

SOME PEOPLE CONFUSE THEIR **SELF-WORTH** WITH THEIR ABILITY TO **ATTRACT THE OPPOSITE SEX**, AND SO POUR ALL THEIR ENERGIES INTO PHYSICAL APPEARANCE— MAKEUP, CLOTHING, JEWELRY, AND THE LIKE.

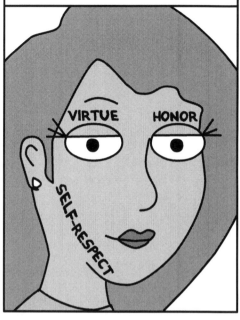

IF ONLY THEY REALIZED THAT **VIRTUE, HONOR,** AND **SELF-RESPECT** ARE THE MARKS OF TRUE BEAUTY!

VIRTUE   HONOR

SELF-RESPECT

XLI

WHEN A PERSON IS OVERLY FOCUSED ON BODILY THINGS— WHETHER OBSESSING OVER FOOD, ENDLESSLY EXERCISING, OR SPENDING HOURS GROOMING—IT BETRAYS THE POVERTY OF THEIR **INTERIOR LIFE.**

CARE FOR YOUR BODY AS NEEDED, BUT PUT MOST OF YOUR ENERGY TOWARDS **CULTIVATING YOUR MIND.**

Mind

34

XLII

WHENEVER SOMEONE HINDERS OR CRITICIZES YOU, REMEMBER THAT THEY CAN ONLY SEE YOU THROUGH THE LENS OF THEIR OWN IMPRESSIONS.

IF THEY'RE SPEAKING OR ACTING FROM A **WARPED PERSPECTIVE**, THEY'RE HURTING THEMSELVES— NOT YOU.

WHEN SOMEONE CONFUSES TRUTH WITH FALSEHOOD, THE **TRUTH** ISN'T HARMED—ONLY THE PERSON WHO'S FALLEN INTO ERROR.

KEEPING THIS IN MIND, TURN AWAY ANY INSULT OR INJURY WITH **KINDNESS**.

IT SEEMS RIGHT TO THEM, BUT THEY'RE MISTAKEN.

XLIII

EVERY SITUATION HAS **TWO HANDLES**—ONE BY WHICH YOU CAN SAFELY CARRY IT, AND ONE THAT'S DANGEROUS TO GRASP.

IF A FRIEND TREATS YOU UNFAIRLY, DON'T TRY TO PICK IT UP BY THE **HANDLE OF REVENGE**,

REACH INSTEAD FOR THE **HANDLE OF RECONCILIATION**. REMEMBER THAT THIS FRIENDSHIP ENRICHES BOTH OF YOUR LIVES, AND THE RELATIONSHIP IS WORTH KEEPING. BY THIS HANDLE, IT CAN BE CARRIED.

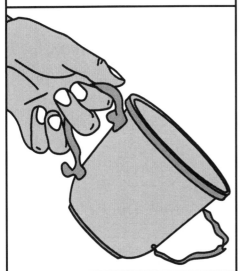

XLIV

HERE ARE SOME EXAMPLES OF **ILLOGICAL CONCLUSIONS:**

I'M RICHER THAN YOU, SO I'M MORE VALUABLE TO SOCIETY.

I'M A BETTER SPEAKER THAN YOU, SO MY OPINION IS MORE IMPORTANT.

THE **LOGICAL CONCLUSIONS** WOULD BE:

I'M RICHER THAN YOU, SO I CAN BUY MORE THINGS.

I'M A BETTER SPEAKER THAN YOU, SO I CAN MORE EASILY SHARE MY OPINIONS.

A PERSON'S **INSIDE** ISN'T MEASURED BY THEIR **OUTSIDE**.

XLV

WHENEVER YOU CATCH YOURSELF **JUDGING** SOMEONE ELSE, **STICK TO THE FACTS**.

DID SOMEONE BATHE QUICKLY? DON'T SAY THAT THEY'RE A SLOB, ONLY THAT THEY WASHED QUICKLY.

DID SOMEONE DRINK A WHOLE BOTTLE OF WINE? DON'T SAY THAT THEY'RE A DRUNKARD, ONLY THAT THEY DRANK A LOT.

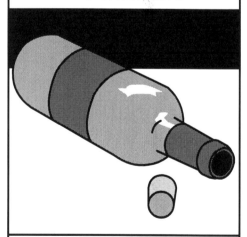

WITHOUT ACCESS TO A PERSON'S **THOUGHTS** AND **MOTIVATIONS**, HOW CAN YOU JUDGE THEM? DON'T MISTAKE YOUR ASSUMPTIONS FOR THE TRUTH.

XLVI

DON'T PROCLAIM YOURSELF A PHILOSOPHER AND GO AROUND PREACHING. SHOW YOUR PRINCIPLES **BY EXAMPLE**.

AT A FEAST, DON'T STAND UP AND GIVE A SPEECH ABOUT MODERATION. JUST PARTAKE MODERATELY YOURSELF.

THIS IS ALL I'M GOING TO DRINK TONIGHT, AND YOU SHOULD DO THE SAME.

SOCRATES NEVER PONTIFICATED OR PUT ON AIRS. IN PHILOSOPHICAL CONVERSATIONS, FOLLOW HIS EXAMPLE—**ASK QUESTIONS** AND **LISTEN MORE THAN YOU SPEAK**.

WHY?

IF ANYONE ASSUMES FROM YOUR SILENCE THAT YOU MUST BE IGNORANT, TAKE IT AS A COMPLIMENT. NOW YOU'RE A TRUE STUDENT OF PHILOSOPHY!

SHEEP DON'T SPIT OUT GRASS TO SHOW THE FARMER HOW MUCH THEY'VE EATEN. THEY **RUMINATE** ON IT, **DIGEST** IT, AND THEN **DISPLAY** THE RESULTS IN WOOL AND MILK.

IN THE SAME WAY, DON'T SPEW YOUR UNDIGESTED IDEAS. SHOW THE FRUITS OF YOUR STUDIES IN **ACTION**.

XLVII

WHEN YOU RESTRAIN YOUR BODILY APPETITES TO GAIN SELF-CONTROL, DON'T BRAG ABOUT IT. AT THE DINNER TABLE, INSTEAD OF ANNOUNCING:

I'VE GIVEN UP WINE, AND SO SHOULD YOU!

JUST SAY:

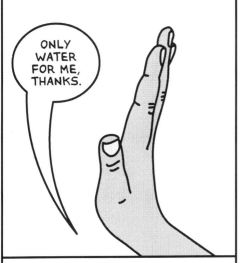

ONLY WATER FOR ME, THANKS.

IF YOU THINK YOU'RE AUSTERE, REMEMBER THE POOR. THEY ENJOY FAR LESS COMFORTS, AND ENDURE FAR GREATER HARDSHIPS, THAN YOU.

DON'T MAKE A SPECTACLE OF YOUR SIMPLICITY, OR YOU DEFEAT THE PURPOSE.

XLVIII

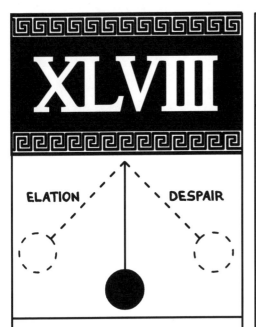

ELATION — DESPAIR

MOST PEOPLE SWING BETWEEN **ELATION** AND **DESPAIR**, TOSSED ABOUT BY THE CURRENTS OF CIRCUMSTANCES AND EVENTS.

BUT PHILOSOPHERS ARE **INTERNALLY ANCHORED**. THEY TAKE RESPONSIBILITY FOR THEIR THOUGHTS AND EMOTIONS. THEY DON'T BLAME ANYONE OR ANYTHING FOR HOW THEY THINK AND FEEL.

THEY LIMIT THEIR STRIVING TO WHAT'S WITHIN THEIR **SPHERE OF POWER**. THEY ACCEPT WHAT'S BEYOND THEIR CONTROL, RATHER THAN FIGHTING IT.

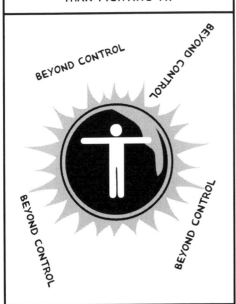

BEYOND CONTROL

THEIR ONLY **ENEMIES** ARE THOSE THINGS WHICH CORRUPT THEIR CHARACTER AND DISRUPT THEIR PEACE OF MIND—LIKE **GREED**, **FEAR**, **ENVY**, AND **HATRED**.

HATRED — FEAR — ENVY — GREED

PEACE

WHEN PHILOSOPHERS FAIL, THEY CORRECT THEIR COURSE. WHEN THEY SUCCEED, THEY SMILE TO THEMSELVES.

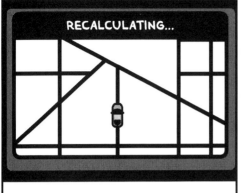

RECALCULATING...

NO MATTER HOW ACCOMPLISHED, THEY CONSIDER THEMSELVES **LIFELONG STUDENTS**— NOT MASTERS.

XLIX

WHEN YOU HEAR A TEACHER BOAST OF BEING ABLE TO UNDERSTAND AND INTERPRET DIFFICULT PHILOSOPHICAL WRITINGS, REMEMBER—IF THE PHILOSOPHERS HAD WRITTEN CLEARLY AND SIMPLY, THERE'D BE NOTHING TO BRAG ABOUT.

WHAT DO I SEEK? TO KNOW THE WAYS OF NATURE. WHO CAN HELP ME KNOW THE WAYS OF NATURE? GREAT PHILOSOPHERS, PRESUMABLY. BUT I CAN'T UNDERSTAND THEIR WRITINGS—WHO CAN HELP ME? TEACHERS AND INTERPRETERS.

WHEN A TEACHER EXPLAINS THE MEANING OF A DIFFICULT TEXT, MY RESPONSE SHOULD BE TO **FOLLOW THE TRUTHS** REVEALED—NOT TO FOLLOW THE TEACHER AS A GURU.

41

THE WHOLE POINT OF **LEARNING** IS TO **LIVE OUT THE TEACHINGS.** THOSE WHO PUT ALL THEIR FOCUS ON READING AND INTERPRETING BOOKS ARE ACADEMICS, NOT PHILOSOPHERS.

L

PRINCIPLE

FOLLOW

ONCE YOU'VE **FOUND** A PRINCIPLE, **FOLLOW IT** AS THOUGH IT WERE A LAW.

DON'T WORRY IF OTHERS CRITICIZE OR LAUGH AT YOU—THEIR OPINIONS AREN'T YOUR CONCERN.

LI

REASON

HOW LONG WILL YOU MAKE EXCUSES FOR NOT PUTTING YOUR PRINCIPLES INTO PRACTICE? HOW LONG WILL YOU WAIT BEFORE FOLLOWING THE **LIGHT OF REASON** WHEREVER IT LEADS?

ARE YOU WAITING TO FIND AN "INFALLIBLE" TEACHER TO GIVE YOU ALL THE ANSWERS? SOME GURU TO WHOM YOU CAN HAND OVER YOUR FREE WILL? YOU'RE RESPONSIBLE FOR YOURSELF—IT'S TIME TO ACT LIKE IT.

IF YOU'RE LAZY OR HALFHEARTED WHEN IT COMES TO PRACTICING PHILOSOPHY, YOU'LL BE **TOSSED** AND **TORMENTED** BY EXTERNAL FORCES TILL YOUR DEATH.

STARTING THIS MOMENT, CHOOSE TO ACT LIKE THE **WORTHY** AND **CAPABLE** PERSON THAT YOU ARE. FOLLOW UNWAVERINGLY WHAT REASON TELLS YOU IS THE BEST COURSE.

TURN RIGHT ON PHILOSOPHY IN 300 FEET.

REASON NAVIGATION

APPROACH LIFE AS YOUR VERY OWN OLYMPIC GAMES. **TRAIN THOROUGHLY** AND **ACT DECISIVELY**—FOR ONE SLIGHT MOVEMENT CAN DETERMINE THE DIFFERENCE BETWEEN VICTORY AND DEFEAT.

LOOK TO SOCRATES—HE CONTINUALLY IMPROVED HIMSELF IN EVERY WAY, WITH REASON AS HIS GUIDE.

OF COURSE, YOU AND I AREN'T SOCRATES. BUT WITH EFFORT, WE CAN ATTAIN THE **SAME VIRTUES** AS SOCRATES.

LII

IN STUDYING PHILOSOPHY,

I THE **FIRST LESSON** IS THE PRACTICAL APPLICATION OF PRINCIPLE.

II THE **SECOND LESSON** IS UNDERSTANDING THE REASONS BEHIND THE PRINCIPLE.

III THE **THIRD LESSON** IS VERIFYING THE PRINCIPLE THROUGH LOGIC.

FOR EXAMPLE, FIRST LEARN AND **LIVE OUT** THE PRINCIPLE OF **HONESTY**.

SECOND, LIST THE **REASONS** WHY TELLING THE TRUTH IS BETTER THAN LYING.

44

THIRD, USE LOGIC TO **PROVE** THAT HONESTY IS THE BEST POLICY.

EACH LESSON IS VALUABLE, BUT THE **FIRST**—PRACTICAL APPLICATION OF PRINCIPLE—IS THE **ESSENTIAL FOUNDATION**.

IN MOST SCHOOLS OF PHILOSOPHY, HOWEVER, THEY SKIP LESSON ONE AND SPEND ALL THEIR TIME DISCUSSING THEORY AND HYPOTHETICALS!

PHILOSOPHY IS FOR LIVING, NOT JUST LEARNING.

LIII

HERE ARE SOME OF MY FAVORITE SAYINGS OF GREAT PHILOSOPHERS:

45

Printed in Great Britain
by Amazon

16811144R00030